THE ART OF THE HUSTLE

MATTIE MALONE'S MEMOIR

Book 1

DEBRAH LYNN PEASE

First Edition: 2026

Published in United States of America

Publisher: *Ebook Writing Experts*

Ebook ISBN	**978-1-966418-19-1**
Paperback ISBN	**978-1-966418-49-8**
Hardcover ISBN	**978-1-966418-41-2**

DEDICATION

The dedication is to all the people who lived a crazy life and wish they had written a book and did not get a chance to write it. This is to all of You!

PROLOGUE

Everyone says truth is stranger than fiction. But not in my world. In my world Truth's just another hustle, and I've become the messenger of time.

I've sold a stick off the ground for ten cents, and I've sold a dream wrapped in stilettos and smoke rings for a whole lot more. My name is Mattie Malone, and this isn't some typical rags-to-riches fairy tale. It's a story engraved in gold, glossed in tequila, and sealed with a kiss. You'll remember the story even after the lipstick fades.

I've made men millionaires and lost more money in a weekend than some people make in a lifetime. I've out talked cops, outlived drug lords, and out danced heartbreak, and sometimes all in one night. But don't mistake me for wild. Everything I've done, I've done with a smile on my face and a plan in my back pocket. You see, I wasn't just chasing money. I was chasing survival, power, and the thrill of knowing that the world couldn't keep up.

There were five husbands. Maybe six. There were love stories that burned hotter than the Texas sun and deals that went colder than the FBI's case files. I've owned restaurants, dodged rats the size of raccoons, hustled with rock stars, and turned fishing trips into criminal close calls. You couldn't make this up if you tried, and Lord knows, I don't have to.

This book is not a confession. It's a celebration.

It is a celebration of wit, of grit, of getting up every time the world tried to knock me down.

So, if you're here for a polished tale with perfect morals, turn back now. But if you're ready to ride shotgun with a woman who lived out loud, laughed in the face of danger, and turned every *"no"* into a new opportunity. You are more than welcome to my world.

Just remember: In Mattie Malone's world, the truth is optional.

But the hustle? That's always real!

ACKNOWLEDGEMENT

To my boyfriend, Chris, thank you for being the first one to tell me that I was a great storyteller, and I should write a book. Your belief in me gave the first spark, and I carried that with me through every chapter of this book.

To Kevin, my Editor, you kept me focused and pushed me to the finish line, and reminded me that rough drafts were just the beginning of something better. I couldn't have done this without your steady guidance.

To all my friends and acquaintances, thank you for listening to me as I rambled on about this character and encouraged me to keep going, and told me again and again to write this book. you helped me believe that it was possible.

To my friends and family, thank you for giving me the peace and quiet and space to put these stories on paper and not being offended when I slipped into Mattie‘s world for days at a time.

And to my girls, Kim, Susie, Lorri, Erica, Jennifer, Amy, and Tabatha, thank you for sticking it out with me through every rough draft pothole and brainstorm. You helped me shape this book into something funny, real, and never told me I was nuts, at least not to my face. I owe you wine, probably lots of it.

To Nick my accomplice and occasional emotional hostage, thanks for loving her, even when she was impossible. you're the steady heartbeat through all this madness that held this all together, and we're all better because you stayed.

To all my husbands of Mattie Malone, some of you were charming, some of you were disasters, and one of you could still be missing. Thanks for playing your part with all this drama. Mattie would not be Mattie without her EX-Files.

And thanks to my son Kevin, who always loves me. I love you with all my heart. And last but not least to Mattie Malone, you burst out on the page with your stilettos, your hustle, your no-apologetic attitude, and refused to let go. And let's be honest, without you, there'd be no story and probably no legal fees either.

And finally, to you, the reader, thank you for picking this book up and flipping it open and walking into Mattie's world, whether you're here for the hustle, the humor, or just trying to figure out how many men she can juggle. I'm glad that you're along for the ride. Just remember, in Mattie's world the truth is optional. But the entertainment is guaranteed.

P.S. The heels get higher, the stakes get hotter, and Mattie's not done talking yet.

Table of Contents

INTRODUCTION

Let me begin by saying I would not be here today without my higher power. I believe God has an alternative reason for my existence in this chaotic world. He has taken me down so many dark paths that I have seen the light at the end of the tunnel.

My mother had a few sayings in life that I was told, which have shaped me into what I am today. She has gone to heaven now; these little sayings are my roots, my ground wire to sanity. The first one, which is oh-so-important, is that *"you are only as pretty as you feel"*.

I've always thought of myself as a positive person. A couple of men in my life have thought the exact opposite—more on that later. I learned early on that the attractiveness of those you meet or are drawn to is reflected in how good you feel about yourself. In other words, wear a smile and keep that smile going, regardless of what occurs, what others say, or what God has in store for you today. Whatever you must do, that *smile* is how you get through it.

You might not feel like smiling because someone has taken advantage of you, put you in a situation you don't want to be in, or lied about you. That smile is what keeps you grounded. It is your *mask*. But if you can keep it planted during all your encounters, you will end up on top of your game.

Every morning, I looked in the mirror, and some days, I didn't wear makeup. I just ran my fingers through my hair, shook my head, and just went for it. But I looked in the mirror every single day, smiled at myself, and said, *"This is it, world! take it or leave it."* That smile was all I had to offer this cruel world that day.

My smile has won hearts. It has gotten me out of many dangerous situations and doors where I should have never entered. That smile has made me someone who attracts people. I'm like a *magnet.* People just want to be near me, not to share me; *they know they want my energy, and my positive thoughts because positive thoughts bring me luck.*

And it's a job—trying to help one feel better, be loved, feel good about oneself, and believe in oneself. To believe it's okay to be as pretty as you feel. Feel good comments, and you look good; *even when you don't feel good, smile and fake it.* You'll have a better day, and those around you will have a better one too.

So, I went into sales. I've sold a lot of things. Well, I can sell anything. Anything that I believe in. I can sell things no one else can, and I can sell you on yourself. Plus, I know how to take charge. Therefore, I've been the boss, the manager. I sold a stick once for ten cents. I took a sales job and part of the training was to sell this stick. If I could sell a twig off the ground, I could sell myself, and then they would know I could sell anything. Next came a string of jobs.

The love of money is powerful, and nothing is more important than making lots of money. I found myself trying to make more and more money — money for my company, money for my products, which put money in my pocket, commission. I just wanted more money — more money than I had on my last job, more money than my boss. I was capable of making lots of money. I just wanted more.

I spent money like there's no tomorrow. I found if you were out of money, you'd find a way to get more and more. I've spent more money in a year than most people make in a lifetime. I pay for my way, and I pay your way, and I don't want it back. I want to spend enough time with you so that you feel you will never forget what we did that day. Something you won't forget, and you will have fun on that day. Money was the ultimate. Spending it on things and times like you had never done before was making an impression on someone—a way not to be forgotten.

I was 16 when I married my first husband. My first husband's minimum wage was 85 cents. *I worked at a doughnut shop for $5 an hour.* Then, I became a telemarketer and employee manager. I brought home 300 a week. It was a short-lived job. The owner moved and closed the business in the middle of the night. Emptied the accounts and tried to skip town. He had made me a signature signer on the business account so I could make out the payroll checks. I had hired most of my friends to be telemarketers, so some were good, some were not.

No one was as good as myself. So, on a Friday I would cash their checks on my lunch hour. This particular week I couldn't cover all the payroll at the bank so I used my personal checking and savings account as collateral. Well the payroll checks bounced and the bank took the funds from my account. My husbands and my personal account. I was devastated. Thousands of dollars were gone, and there was no boss to explain. So, my dad and my husband's dad went to find the boss.

After a late night of hunting him down they took him to the bank the next morning where he signed promissory notes with the bank to pay all the money back and release the obligation from me and return my money. We never saw him again. What a lesson I had to learn about trusting people at such an early age. That wasn't my first job though, my first job, I was 15 and worked 6pm to 9pm. I gave dinners away as a telemarketer at exquisite restaurants. (Dunston's steak house was one of the free dinners and Dunston's has a billboard out front of it today thanking Dallas Texas, for sixty years of serve.)

We had lots of contests to give us an incentive to book these appointments. They pinned concert tickets on the wall, and whoever booked the most appointments won the tickets. I booked 100 appointments that night. We sat in very small cubicles with a mirror right in front of our face. We looked in this mirror all night while we called people from a list, a Cole directory. There was a sign above the mirror that said, *"Smile and dial"* they proved that if you spoke with a smile on your face, not a frown, that it sold your product, and they were right. It was my start of proving facts. Smiling brings positive.

Positive brings sales. And sales bring money. That was my first time dealing with commission. And commission jobs were where the money was. I would bring home $200 at that job for 15 hours a week. Minimum wage was 85 cents an hour. And I saw commission sales was my forte'. But I wanted to sell things my way not theirs. So, I became the boss and I trained those under me how to sell. And it went back to what my mother had said: keep a smile on your face, *"You are only as pretty as you feel."*

My mother also told me, *"Never tell a man the whole story. Tell him all of the story but the end, and then he'll always be back tomorrow to hear the end. When you can start a new story, he will return day after day to hear the story."*

So now I am writing this book. I hope you like Mattie Malone and some of her many adventures. Thanks for believing in me.

CHAPTER 1

MIMOSAS, MONEY, AND MATTIE'S WORLD

This story starts where most end. She's sitting at an outside table that overlooks the sea, very close to the swimming pool at the Morosa Hotel in beautiful Costa Rica. She's alone for a change, just sipping her mimosa and playing with the little umbrella that came in the drink. She's mesmerized by the sound of the sea and the beauty of the colors across the sky from the sun, which is about to set.

She'd thought of each of her husbands she had, giving each one a couple of minutes. Only to take her deeper into her mesmerized thoughts. Mattie was 45 now and had just lost her fourth husband to cancer about 3 months ago. She never loved Ed like the others she had been married to. Nevertheless, she was married to Edward for 3 years, and the last 2 years were a *nightmare.*

Edward was older than Mattie by 15 years. He had been married four times before Mattie was his fifth. Mattie had been friends with Edward's wife for years when Melanie got sick and, eventually, at an early age, died of alcohol poisoning. *That* left Edward alone.

He and Melanie could not have any children. Edward had a vasectomy when he was 25; *he had no family to carry on his name.* Years later, after Melanie's death, Edward looked Mattie up and pleaded with her to come to his side, saying that he was ill and expected to die soon, and Mattie eventually said, *"Yes."*

Mattie had left the state years before she needed a change. She was a spontaneous type of woman and loved a good adventure, especially if money was involved. Money was how the world went around to Mattie. You are nobody without cash, and Mattie spent every day thinking of ways to get more money.

Mattie used her mind to make money. She rose every morning of her life thinking of ways to make money, hopefully *legally*. The amount of money was the most important thing. Then, what it cost others was the last item on her list.

Hopefully, you never crossed Mattie; *she would make you the last thing on her list.* But before you knew it, you'd be making money alongside Mattie. She always got the larger percentage of the money you were making.

Her marriage to Edward wasn't about *love,* but about *obligations, loyalty, and companionship*. Mattie was an impulsive type of woman, especially if money was involved. Mattie came up with a way to make money that other people never thought of, and she would cut you in on the same deal if she liked you. Even shared her wealth with those she hung out with. It was Mattie's way of not feeling guilty about how she managed to receive this money.

Mattie had a *cunning* nature. As she focused on money, she was compelling and morally complex. It made you wonder if this drive for money affected her marriages for their moments when it put her in trouble or pushed her into morally gray territory. Her ambition and complex morality shaped her decisions and relationships. Her schemes worked *brilliantly*.

Casting her cleverness and resourcefulness and sometimes her pursuit of money led to trouble or unintended circumstances and consequences. Maybe even betrayal or losses. How her perspective of money evolved over time? and she eventually realized the cost of always putting money first. Maybe Mattie saw money as a survival tool, and she never let go of it.

Mattie was fair as long as you were fair to her, but if you hadn't been, the penalty would be at a high interest rate. Maybe even with some deadlines on paying her back. Mattie came into money more often than a school boy has dated. Mattie came into tens of thousands of dollars at a time. I remember her coming into a $120,000 at one time. It was spent in less than 3 to 4 weeks. Mattie could spend it faster than she could get it.

But Mattie was an entrepreneur. There were many times, she was told by others, *"Let me go into business with you. I want to be by your side and make money like you do."* But Mattie got bored too easily to take on a partner in any business adventure she got into. She would come up with an idea and invite only the ones she needed to fulfill her scheme. Sometimes, those who knew her the best were scared to participate, because Mattie had a lot of guts.

She pushed herself where no one had pushed before. And 9 out of 10 times, or even 10 out of 10, she came out on top, smelling like a rose.

Mattie's relationship with money isn't just about greed or luxury. It's about *survival*, and this drives her actions and decisions of desperation and calculated coldness in some situations. It's a belief system for her. It shapes her worldview and interaction with others. Her survival, mentally, pushes her to take drastic measures, possibly even hurting relationships. Perhaps she justifies her choices by telling herself that in a world that demands money to survive, the ends justify the means.

Mattie stays firm in her belief that money is the key to survival, and nothing will ever sway her, especially with people who might value love, loyalty, or honesty over wealth, not my Mattie.

With only money on her mind, it came with a price, as all money does. It caused deeper emotional connections. Her past marriages might reflect on this. Her partners loved her but couldn't compete with her obsession with financial security. This adds a darker edge to Mattie's character. When she might manipulate or outsmart people to get ahead, she never looks back or second-guesses herself. I'm not sure I have enough time to tell you about all of these money excursions, but a few of the biggest ones are what gave Mattie her *reputation.*

So, as she sat looking at the sea drinking her mimosa, I pulled up a chair and asked her what was on her mind. She looked over at me with those big blue, dreamy eyes. She had the longest eyelashes—every one of them was natural. She smiled, a *smile* that made you melt. She could make you feel like you were the only person in the room. You felt as if she was part of you.

Mattie was a people person. She can make anyone think they are the most special man or woman to her. That you felt as if she was part of you. Your consciousness made you feel loved, important, and needed. The needed part was her talent, she made everyone feel they needed her. It was a knack she had. You would do almost anything to win her attention. She had a big heart. She was a force to be reckoned with, someone who had calculated confidence and was in control of every situation, no matter how challenging.

She always stayed one step ahead. Navigating the complexity of her life with precision. Her confidence could create friction with those around her. People might admire or resent her for it. She could also have an aura of invincibility making it even more intriguing when the world of people around her shift in ways she can't predict. Her control remains unshaken always coming out on top.

She laid her hand palm up for me and said, *"You know me oh so well. I'm thinking about money for my next adventure."*

Mattie and I had known each other for almost 30 years, 26 to be exact. Mattie still associated with people she had known for longer than that. Hell, she married two of her best friends, and I now was her best friend, but we kept it open. I'm not sure I could live up to her many expectations. But I would give it my best shot if she wanted to try.

Mattie and I were in Costa Rica, spending the money she had left from her marriage to Edward. She always fitted the bill wherever she went. She always said, *"Many can't afford to do what I want to do."* So, she would pay and off we would go. Hanging with Mattie was something you would never forget or ever want to miss. She went to the most extravagant places always looking for a fun time.

Mattie keeps her friends at arm's length. That way, no new acquaintances get to tag along. You had to know Mattie for years, before she would fight for you, before she took you into her world. The world, let's say, that no man would travel again, without Mattie.

I remember once, when Mattie was in her early thirties, she was married to *Rick*. Rick was messing with some heavy characters. Most of whom were illegal back then. When I say illegal, I'm talking about the sale of *drugs.*

Mattie and Rick sold marijuana. Back then, you went to prison for just having one marijuana cigarette in your possession. That didn't sway Mattie from seeing all the money that was involved. They started small, seeing the profit in a bag of marijuana was unbelievable. They could buy a large bag of green leafy stuff and share the price with a couple of friends, and it would pay for itself with money left over. *A lot of money.*

So, the bags or packages got bigger, and their friends got new friends, and the green leafy stuff started coming in from all around: *Mexico, Arizona, California,* and even *Bogota, Peru.* The packages were coming in by truckloads.

Mattie and Rick were getting 10 lbs. at a time. They could make 2 to 3 pounds. of profit out of each 10 pounds, making it 12 to 13 pounds. Mattie realized the potential was in the $100,000. No matter how much you smoked off the green sticky stuff, you cannot smoke your profit away. The money started flowing in. Mattie and Rick owned their own home, but it was not feasible to live in the suburbs. The big city was the place to be, *right in the heart of the party.* And that was where Mattie wanted to be. That's where the money was, and that's also where they would meet their best contacts.

Mattie was shrewd and resourceful, operating in a world of strict terms and calculations. It's *clear* she used her intelligence to navigate both money and relationships. Her fairness with those who are fair to her but unforgiveness with those who cross her, adds complexity to her moral code. Her ability to spend money as fast as she makes it shows her impulsive side despite her otherwise controlled demeanor.

This could reflect a deeper hunger or need for something she can't fulfill with money alone. There's a sense that money isn't just a tool for survival for Mattie. It's also a way to feel powerful, even in ways that are almost reckless. She seems unstoppable; *she thrives on a challenge and the thrill of control.* Mattie is not just about money. She needs excitement, and that comes from being in complete control. She never really makes people her equal. She keeps everything at arm's length; *her drive isn't just for wealth. It's for power and independence.*

I remember going out with Rick and Mattie one night, and we were doing the usual, and getting all dolled up to hit the town. Mattie had a top on that had lights on it. Mattie's mother had returned from *Las Vegas* with a gift for her daughter, Mattie. It was a black lace top with tiny red lights that flashed on and off. It was very *sexy. Yet,* everyone would not miss the person who wore it.

She stood out across the room. And in a dark bar, she was *illuminating.* Those little red lights flickered off and on. The lights took up the whole front of her chest, from her breasts to her waist. They were in an outline of a glass of champagne, with the tiny bubbles coming from it. *Boy, how she shone.* Anyone would have been embarrassed to be so illuminating, but not *Mattie.* She held her head high, put that oh-so-beautiful smile on her face, and walked in like she was the owner of the place. Like no one was there but her and the person whom she was headed for.

"Just you and her."

Mattie had her arm through her husband's arm and held my hand, so gently on her other side, and in we went. You knew every eye in the place was staring at her with that top twinkling those little red lights. Mattie saw a table off to the side where we could sit. After about 30 minutes of drinking and getting to know our surroundings, Mattie took off for the ladies' room. You never let Mattie go by herself; *she might meet someone or find someone she wants to know.* It might be a while before she would return, and this night was no different. Mattie returned with this man, who was a bit older than we were.

He was so infatuated with Mattie. He sat down and introduced himself. His name was *Stoney Burns.* The *Stoney Burns!* He had written an underground newspaper in Dallas, Texas, in the late sixties to early seventies. He was quite a well-known guy in the underground. We knew he was friends with many influential characters. Well, some might not be so legal. He was always in the Dallas newspapers for getting involved with the police. They had it out for Stoney. That night, Stoney wanted to party with Mattie, so off we went.

Stoney left Mattie's at about 7 a.m. We never heard from him again. It was a night of Cocaine. But at that time, he drove a convertible with graffiti all over it. It sat outside Mattie's house until dawn that morning. *I wonder what the neighbors thought. They were used to it, I thought!*

Despite the allure of her warmth and attention, Mattie's focus remained on her next move, her next win. This reinforces that she always looks ahead, never truly present in the moment. For anyone else, her ability to make people feel needed and her big heart are what keeps people invested in her, even when they know the game she's playing.

Back then, Mattie and Rick were into many different things. They both worked regular jobs, but their side job was selling *marijuana.* They knew some Colombians who wanted American goods, so they set up a deal of one planeload of pot for a shipment of those American items.

When I talk about American items, I'm talking about eight pairs of *size-seven cowboy boots, eight Texas Longhorns* mounted on the wall, *eight sets of washers* and *dryers, eight dishwashers,* and *eight cowboy hats.* With that, the plane load was theirs. The second that plane loaded, the FBI was waiting, and everyone went down except for Mattie and Rick. They produced *eight-by-ten glossies* of the whole operation in court. There were other close calls, but Mattie just put it out of her mind and trudged forward.

CHAPTER 2

ENCOUNTERING WITH ROCK LEGENDS

Mattie was in school when a school dance was coming up, and the school had arranged for a band to play for the dance.

She thought the band was a local band with local musicians; *the members were just a couple of years older than Mattie.* The musicians were good, and the dance was a success. Later in life, Mattie was told about the musicians. They went to a private boy's school down the road from Mattie's school. The two members, in particular, were two guys who started a garage band together; that's what they called it back then. The group's leader and singer was a guy known as *Steve Miller.* And the second musician was *Boz Skaggs.*

Both guys grew up to have bands of their own. As we know now, the Steve Miller Band is very successful, having cut several gold records through his career and is still going strong. He was known for songs like *Abracadabra, Take the Money and Run, Fly Like an Eagle, and All Right Now,* just to name a few.

Boz Skaggs went on to have his own group. Independently, he was known for songs like *Lowdown, Lido Shuffle, and Who's That Lady.* Both are still making money today as musicians.

Mattie will not let you forget that she experienced these times with the rock stars. She even tells a tale of her husband, Rick. He was working as an appliance tech (*dishwashers, clothes machines, and refrigerators*). He had gotten a service call at a residence near where he and Mattie had gone to school. The houses were in a very high-class neighborhood.

Rick went on a service call to fix a woman's dishwasher that was under warranty. When he arrived, a friendly woman invited him in while trying to correct the problem, a woman chattered to Rick, making it impossible to do his job.

This woman kept going on and on about her son. He had done this, moved here, come back, and on and on. She would not stop chattering the whole time. Rick worked until he finally fixed the dishwasher and told the lady he needed the breaker box in the house.

The woman said, *"Sure, it's in the master bedroom closet; follow me."*

Rick was so glad he had given the woman something to do to quiet her down for a minute. As he followed her through the beautifully decorated living room and started down the long hall to the master bedroom, Rick noticed these vinyl records on the hall's walls. After a couple of minutes, he couldn't pass another without stopping to look, and the vinyl albums were golden in color.

He studied the label a little closer, and the album was by an artist named Steve Miller Band. *The Steve Miller Band, he thought?* He remembered hearing the lady say, *"Stevie is doing this and that."* After he flipped the breaker and returned to the kitchen, he pulled up a chair, and the lady began to tell him all about her son again. Now that Rick became so interested, Rick stayed way after the appointment just to hear what all the lady had to tell him about her famous son.

Rick could not wait to get home that night to tell Mattie he was in the home of the Steve Miller Band today. He sat with Steve's mom and saw Steve Miller's gold records lining the hall. *What a day.*

When Rick told Mattie, she couldn't wait to tell everyone. Mattie would tell the tale, *"As the years went on, making you think she was present that day in Steve Miller's mom and dad's home."* Mattie kept you on the edge with her stories, and this tale was only the *beginning.*

Mattie loved music. Listening to the radio in her car was her thing. She would turn it up loud and dance while driving, singing along, knowing most of the words. When she didn't, she'd never let you know. Mattie's first husband, Tony, was a drummer, and he mainly taught Mattie about instruments, such as guitars and drums. She knew her *Gibson's, Stratocasters, Fenders, and Flying V's.*

Her drums were *Ludwig* and *Slingerland* back then. There are many drums today, but those are the ones Tony taught her about. Tony was so long ago that we don't hear much about him. But I'm sure we will soon!

CHAPTER 3

RESTAURANT VENTURE

Mattie's next adventure was a *restaurant.* She and Rick bought a café. They redid it inside and out, and Mattie saw dollar signs. Rick started out as the cook and used recipes from Mattie: *homemade chicken-fried steak, meatloaf, fried fish, and fried okra.* The restaurant did very well, and they bought a second location and called it something different. Rick traveled back and forth from one to the other.

The second restaurant was robbed twice at night when it was closed. Rick got a partner to stake out the crooks. Before they could catch the crooks, there was a fire next door, and the soot ruined all the restaurant decor. Mattie was *sick.* The plants burned, and the white tablecloths were ruined. That was when Mattie left the restaurant business and went back to her old job of selling gold. Her boss had come to the restaurant and had offered Mattie $25000 a year to return to her job. So she jumped at that money. Rick sold both restaurants, and they were deep into the marijuana business full-time.

I remember going to Mattie's one Friday night. It was clear outside: *you could see every star in the sky.* As I walked into the house, this thick fog mist was overwhelming. It looked like smoke and smelled like the sweetest marijuana brownies.

I asked Mattie what was up with all this, and she said, *"Rick must be bagging tonight. "As we climbed the stairs in the duplex, the fog got thicker and thicker. We opened the spare room door; through the fog sat three grown men. Each looked a little scruffy.*

Pounds of marijuana lined the wall behind them. Shower curtain liners laid on the floor beneath them to protect the carpet from all the marijuanna.

Triple-beam scales glimmered off the glass table in the room. Rick had moved up. He had received 150 pounds this time. It came in three big bricks weighing fifty pounds each. The bricks had to be broken up and misted with water to hold the pot together and add weight to the marijuana itself. Rick pulled 10 pounds out of each 50 pounds brick as profit. *That's 30 pounds of pure profit.*

Mattie wanted this money but didn't want the risk it brought. Mattie and I headed to the bar, but she was always one step ahead. She decided to rent a separate apartment to store all this pot in it instead of their personal residence. The pounds sold for $1,100 a pound. They owed $45,000 for the marijuana. But $165,000 was to be made on the retail side. Rick's guy was a businessman. He gave Rick three months to pay him. Mattie told me they paid him in six weeks.

The profit was unbelievable. With that, everyone decided to go on vacation. Rick went snow skiing with his friends, and Mattie visited friends in Colorado with her friends. Rick got to party in Jimmy Buffett's house, swimming in the hot tub and doing drugs. And Mattie, well, *she was a celebrity.*

CHAPTER 4

ADVENTURES OF COLORADO

Colorado was a good vacation for Mattie. She had a male friend from school who had three male roommates: *blonde, brunette,* and *many muscles.* Mattie was great with strangers. She had never met a stranger with whom she could not make a quick connection, and this time was no different.

With that, she and two friends headed by car to Colorado. Mattie took the wheel first, while the two women stated they could not drive a four-speed. Mattie drove until she felt completely exhausted. The car she would leave in fourth gear, and one would switch seats with her at 60 mph so that she could get a little nap.

"Just keep the pedal to the floor," she said.

Mattie had gotten into the back seat. It seemed like 30 minutes went by, and the car started jerking, waking her up. The girls had reached the mountains, and they needed to downshift the car, and they didn't know how. They pulled the car over on the shoulder, and Mattie had to resume being the driver. They opened a bottle of *sangria wine* and began to pass it back and forth among them. The girls were happy they had gotten Mattie up. *She was the life of every party.*

They arrived in Aspen, Colorado, right before dark. Her friend had instructed Mattie that the four men lived in a trailer over the railroad tracks, being the first one on the left. The key to the door was under the flowerpot on the porch. Her friend's old Monte Carlo, the silver one, would be parked in front. So, they went over the tracks, and there was a trailer. A silver Monte Carlo was parked there. However, this trailer was very small. *How did four men live in this?*

The girls parked, and the key was under the pot. They opened the door and went inside, laughing the whole time. Mattie spun around once inside, and she let out a little scream. *"What the hell is this?"* she yelled. There was no way for those four men to live in this cracker box.

They started looking around. This was a travel trailer, not a mobile home. Mattie felt like she had been tricked. There was one bedroom. *How would they all fit?* Paul was a very old and good friend of Mattie's. *Why would he have told her there was plenty of room?* That each man had his own bedroom.

She thought this was the wrong place, so she told the women to look around and find something that belonged to Paul to prove it was his place. During their search, one of them opened the oven, and to their surprise, the stove held a rolling tray. On the rolling tray, there was a large amount of loose marijuana and a pack of papers. They all began to laugh. Mattie sat down, rolled a joint, and lit it.

Discuss how small this place was, how the men could not fit very well, and how the women wouldn't fit with them unless they all stood up. They all begin to laugh, they plan to stay for five days, which would not work out in their favor *at all.* They almost smoked the whole joint when Mattie decided to roll another for the road, and they would just drive around to see if the girls could find another place nearby.

Mattie was exhausted from driving the entire trip by herself. She just wanted a nap before all the men got off from work and the Aspen party began. They loaded up, and off they went. They found some cabins to rent not far away on the river. It was beautiful, the river rushing and cold. Two bedrooms, with a kitchen and dishes—*perfect.* Mattie took a shower and quickly fell asleep.

The cabin was cozy, and the girls made a fire in the fireplace and started dinner. *Tacos* would be a quick and easy meal; they would let Mattie sleep. Right at 8 PM, there was a banging at the door. It woke Mattie, in bursted Paul.

Panting and raving, *"Where is Mattie?"* he shouted.

Mattie came out of the bedroom, and her hair was a mess. As she wore her lacy PJs. They were low-cut on the top and very see-through. Paul's mouth dropped open when he rushed toward Mattie, scooping her in his arms. He spun her around a couple of times, then set her down in his lap on the couch and started in on her.

"What are you doing here? I've been looking all over town for you. No one said they had seen you." He went on.

Mattie said, *"Well, honey, that place of yours is not big enough for our clothes. We three could not sleep in there. I don't know how four grown men can live in that cracker box."*

Paul looks shocked. Silence comes next. He stood up and said, *"Too small? It's a four-bedroom."*

The girls started laughing, and Mattie began to explain where they were.

Paul laughed and said, *"Woman, you were in the wrong house!"*

Mattie explained the flowerpot, the key, the Monte Carlo, and the oven findings.

"Hey girl, pass the trailer park, then turn left on the first road at the bottom of the hill," Paul said.

"It's a lonely trailer on the river; it sits all alone. Come on and get this stuff packed up, and I'll take you," he said. It didn't take long to load everything up; Mattie knew Paul would find her. So she got dressed, then Paul loaded the car, and they went looking for the trailer.

They had passed several other trailers. Then, there was a road. They took a left, and a trailer was at the bottom of the drive, beautifully located and it was all alone at the bottom of that hill.

Paul was right. It is very secluded, sitting right on the riverbanks. It was beautiful down there, and here we are, three other men sitting on the porch, waiting for Paul to return with the women.

CHAPTER 5

DECAMPING OF HIGH-STAKES

As we all knew, Mattie was no stranger to men, and the vacation to Colorado was a *hit.* Mattie came home to her husband, who was planning a trip to the Bahamas with a married couple they had partied with for years.

Dave made good money, and *Theresa* was a Montessori school teacher. They did very well financially and could almost keep up with Mattie and her husband.

The four were inseparable for a couple of years. Then David and Theresa split up. They had no children and owned their own home with a pool in the backyard. They were a little freaky, but Mattie loved them. They were also different from typical couples; *I guess that's what kept them from getting bored with each other.*

Theresa loves using cocaine. Both partners tried to hide this fact from each other. Theresa calls Mattie on her day off to make plans without the guys, and Dave calls Mattie when Theresa isn't around. The two of them kept Mattie hopping. This was the very early '80s when cocaine was good.

It wasn't as expensive as it is today. Before, they would get together on a Saturday afternoon, do a little sunbathing and swimming, then go to an expensive place for dinner. Like the *Turtle Creek* restaurant or the *Bachman Lake* seafood restaurant, they would have stuffed *snapper,* one of Mattie's favorites.

They also ate at Southern Kitchen. They were very exclusive servings, a 5 — to 7-course meal. Sometimes, they would even rent a limo to drive around in.

They started making plans to go to the Bahamas. Mattie and Hubby had been to the Bahamas twice before. Mattie thought it was so beautiful.

The perfect ocean—no waves, crystal clear—was all too perfect. No one had children to attend to, so time—what they called time—was on their side. They went shopping, gambling, parasailing, and deep-sea fishing.

Mattie was trying to think ahead, So on the day they went deep sea fishing, she went to the market in The Bahamas and made sandwiches for everyone on the boat, about 12 people. Little did she realize that she had made tuna sandwiches, and every one of those fishermen and fisherwomen got sick, throwing up all over that deep-sea fishing boat.

That was quite a day. The fish they caught were cleaned, cooked, and served at the fish fry that night on the beach at the *Holiday Inn hotel.* It was very nice in 1981. During the fish fry, the hotel had prepared big bonfires on the beach. After dinner, everyone made their way to the sand, and that's when it *happened.*

All these bricks were wrapped in black trash bags and floated up on the beach. Each bag was the size of a kilo. A kilo is 2.2 pounds. Kilos of the best Colombian redbud marijuana. There were at least 50 to 100 kg everywhere on the beach. People started ripping open the bags to find real Redbud marijuana, and the party got started.

The other hotel down the beach got other black bags at their bonfire—bags of cocaine. The two hotel patriots traded their treasures with each other until the police showed up. Grabbing handfuls, everyone headed for their rooms. The four were *ecstatic.*

The men got the women quiet, and the private party started. Once on the plane home, people were talking about the packages that floated up the beach and how the cops came. Mattie and her three companions sat quietly in their seats, not wanting anyone to know they had escaped that night with handfuls.

David and Rick closed their eyes, pretending to be asleep as the plane loaded with people and the stories went on and on. Mattie and Theresa's lips curled up, just sitting there with big grins on their faces trying not to burst out; they got away again.

CHAPTER 6

YACHTS, GUM, AND MISADVENTURES

Mattie had a friend named *Renee*, who was younger than Mattie, but she came from money. Renee's parents had a couple of boats at the marina, and Renee invited Mattie out on her 30th birthday. Mattie wasn't sure about spending this memorable birthday with Renee. She had hoped for a big celebration, yet no one had planned anything for her this year. She was disappointed.

She just waited until the last minute to accept Renee's offer. Now, Renee tried to entice Mattie with her *best-selling* points, and the first was something Mattie wanted to see.

Renee told Mattie her family had a Sky Lift to the boat. In the marina parking lot, there was a Sky Lift. This lift only used by Renee's family at their boat dock. It was sealed off at the boat dock, and no other boat dock patrons could enter it. Mattie agreed, and off they went, just the two women on this birthday adventure.

The girls drove about an hour and a half out of town to the lake. They started around 10 PM; Mattie's birthday would begin at midnight, and they wanted a full day of celebrating. Once they arrived, it was dark, but as Renee had said, there was a Sky Lift. They just got in the gondola and rode out in the dark to the dock. Once on the dock, it was just as she had told Mattie. The dock had a door at each end of the slip, but they were padlocked shut. So, the girls left them locked.

There were two large boats in the slips of that boat dock. Mattie wasn't sure of her lengths, but 50 to 60 feet was an understatement. Mattie knew that most boats she had ever been on had two or three steps when you went down below, and this boat had seven or eight. The slips had electricity, and the two boats were so elegant.

Mattie was in *awe*. The larger of the two was Renee's parent's boat, and the other was her uncle's. Her dad's brother. And like the TV show, her dad's name was *Bobby*, and her uncle's name was *J.R,* but their last name was not *Ewing;* Mattie thought that was so *funny*.

The two men's families shared the dock, and they had about five refrigerators on the dock, between the two boats. Just in case someone did break into the fridge, it had chains and padlocks all around each of them, too. The girls brought their own ice chest with drinks, as food was not on their list.

Renee gave Mattie a tour of the largest boat. It was beautiful—all the decks were shining, looking brand new and unused. She was on board pretending to be the captain, hanging onto the wheel like she was driving the boat, laughing and cutting up. Then they went downstairs. There was a large open area with a couch, chairs, a coffee table, and a wet bar. *Mirrors* were everywhere, and it was immaculate, bright, and shiny. It was *beautiful*.

Now, Mattie had known from the experience of going down below on other boats that the ship's point was usually the bed you walked downstairs and landed on the bed, not having much room to do anything else but lie down. But this downstairs was *different*.

It featured a *king-size* bed flanked by a nightstand on either side. It was illuminated—there was so much light—and the boat was perfectly covered with a bright designer bedspread and many throw pillows. Standing below the deck, you could see this spectacular view. There was ample space. Mattie had never stood up in a boat when she went below, but this boat was *stunning*.

Renee had not given it a fair shot. She had not bragged about these yachts. Just the opposite, really; she had never spoken of these gorgeous treasures before, and they were still unexplored but extravagant. Renee was not as impressed as Mattie. Her stomach fluttered just looking at all the shining, glittering objects below. Mattie was scared to touch anything. Feeling uncomfortable around this magnificent boat, Renee took her back up top, and they stepped off the yacht and onto the dock.

The second boat was a bit smaller, but just as elegant as the one she had just exited. This was a whole new level of luxury, and she wasn't sure if she could handle it. The thought of messing up or looking foolish in front of Renee made her hesitant, but as always, she didn't let that show. Instead, she tried to act confident, smiling as if it were another day on the water. Renee, noticing Mattie's tension, reassured her with an easy smile.

For a moment, Renee must have seen Mattie's worrisome face because she quickly said, *"Hey, Mattie, come look on the other side of the boat. This is the boat I thought we could take out."* Hanging on the side of the elegant yacht was a 21-foot ski boat. Mattie was accustomed to this kind of boat, and her eyes lit up instantly.

Renee said it was no big deal to lower this ski boat into the lake and detach it from the bigger boat, and that was what the girls did. It was about 3 AM now, and the girls wanted to fish, so they decided to open up the ice chest and get started on the birthday.

They hadn't thought about a bait. But there were some hot dogs in the fridge that they could cut up and use, and that's what they did. Neither wanted to touch a live worm or nightcrawler, as they were called. They got some lawn chairs and sat on the edge of the dock. They talked, laughed, and teased each other for a couple of hours.

Mattie was a livid gum chewer; before the fishing ended, she decided to spit her gum out and into the lake. All of a sudden, two fish appeared to eat the gum. The girls looked at each other and started to laugh. Mattie had lots of gum in her purse, so they began to put several pieces in their mouths at a time, making a big wad of gum. Then, it went straight to the hook. The fish began to bite. Renee was the first to catch one, followed by Mattie, who also reeled in a fish after feeling the tug.

The girls were unsure what kind of fish they were catching or what they would do with the caught fish. They just let them go again, and the fish loved the gum, and the girls' drug in more fish. They chuckled about the number of fishermen who would never think of using gums. They concluded that there were too many, bursting into even more laughter. So, just like typical women, after a couple of fish each, they had conquered fishing, were bored, and wanted more excitement. They decided to take the ski boat out.

Renee had done this before because she knew exactly what to do. Mattie waited patiently while Renee lowered the dinghy into the water. Mattie was impressed that Renee knew so much about taking this boat down, from hanging in the slip to lowering it into the lake and detaching it from the larger boat.

Once in the water and ready to load, the girls got their ice chests and climbed into the smaller ski boat. The boat was not just a little dingy. It was a bigger ski boat than most of the ones Mattie had owned or skied on. It, too, looked brand new.

Mattie had partied on a 38-foot Chris Craft 1 Summer, and a friend of her mom's owned it. It was all wood, and Mattie had swabbed the deck on that boat, trying to shine it up. It had three steps going down below, and it had a bed below, but you could not stand up, nor did it have a nightstand or living room. Just a bed, a bath, and some small fridges.

It was a large boat to Mattie. One Saturday morning, she put a hundred dollars in the gas tank to go out on the 38-foot Chris Craft that weekend. The gas gauge did not even come off empty. She remembered wondering how much it would cost to fill the boat up. Renee's dad owned a yacht three times the size of the boat that Mattie partied on that one summer years ago.

Mattie asked Renee about the gas in the ski boat, and Renee said it was full, so off the girls went. It was dawn now, and the sun was coming up as they left the boat slip. Renee drove, and she was a woman who liked to drive fast; *the boat was no different.* They rode around the shores of the lake for quite a few minutes before stopping to take in a little sun and talk to each other over the loud sound the boat made while they were moving.

Once they stopped the boat and got ready to sunbathe, Mattie noticed a little water on her feet that wasn't there before. She mentioned this to Renee, and she got alarmed, saying there should not be any water in the boat. And then it dawned on Renee. She had not put the plug in the boat. So frantically, the girls started looking for some help.

They had seen a lot of boats going out on the lake that morning. This lake was known for its fishermen. It was half on the Texas side and half on the Oklahoma side. The shore was beautiful on the Oklahoma side—white sand. The girls had rowed on the lake for a while, and they could not see the dock. They started yelling at any boat they could. And the ski boat was now ankle-deep. Mattie had not thought of the consequences yet, but Renee had.

She began telling Mattie they needed to find help fast, and yelling at the boats driving by was not helping. They could not hear them over their engines roaring. Mattie could see many boats, but they were too far away to hear. As the boat kept taking on water, standing at the front of the boat, yelling was not getting their attention. As the boat was getting deeper in the water, they was not getting any boat's attention.

Mattie started to think, and then it came to her. They needed to get the boat's attention. She said to Renee, *"Renee, take off your shirt, stand on the nose of the boat, and wave your arms."* Both girls pulled their shirts over their heads and began to wave their arms, and no kidding, the boats started coming their way.

Three boats arrived at the same time. The girls started explaining, and the men started arguing. When Renee got mad and screamed, *"Shut up! My grandfather is Pappy of Pappy's Bait Shop, and he will pay anyone who gets us and the boat back to the dock."* Then, the men decided which boat would pull us to safety.

Once the boats arrived, the girls put their shirts back on, and the boat owners helped them aboard their fishing boat. They tied on the ski boat, and to the dock they headed. Upon getting to the dock, the ski boat was barely seen above the water. The men tied the boat to the dock for the girls. And they left the sinking boat.

Mattie just knew they were in big trouble. Three-fourths of the boat was under the water. But Renee did not seem that worried. She gathered their stuff, and they hurried to the sky lift to get to the car. Once at the car, the bait shop was not far from the marina they were at. Renee told her to wait in the car while she ran inside.

Renee was not inside long; she was back in the car, saying the guy at the bait shop would take care of everything. He would take a pump down to the dock, pump all the water out, and then sell the boat. Mattie couldn't believe that they were just going to drive off and leave this problem they had created for someone else to fix, but the girls had no idea what they would have done except let the boat sink. Oh, what a day this was.

They had almost two hours to get home; *by then, it was late afternoon.* Mattie hopes to do something more tonight for her birthday, that the girls need to nap and prepare for the evening. Once they were off, Renee explained to Mattie that her grandpa would take care of everything, there was nothing to worry about. Another adventure had been accomplished, Mattie thought.

CHAPTER 7

A LIFE WITH UNWANTED GUEST

They both were staying at Renee's. She had a single-wide trailer her parents had bought her. Renee had told Mattie she could stay there until she got on her feet. Mattie had just left her second husband, and divorce was inevitable.

Renee had a two-bedroom trailer in a park. It was new and had a larger lot than the other trailers. However, it had one *drawback*.

Renee said a mouse had moved in, and her parents hired an exterminator to get rid of it. However, the exterminator said he couldn't find the mouse when he came out. He did, however, mention that the mouse was probably now a rat that had eaten a whole 50-lb. bag of dog food.

Renee said she knew he was coming into the trailer because he was taking cigarette butts out of the ashtray when she came home for lunch.

One night, Mattie had a few friends over to the trailer. They were having tequila shots in the living room when a huge rat showed up. He sat up on his hind legs like a begging dog, and that was the first time he was seen.

A month had passed, and Mattie and Renee had set traps for the rat, using peanut butter to lure him to the trap. But this mouse was *smart*; he would lick the peanut butter down to the last lick before the trap went off. The game continued.

The following Sunday, the girls were going to watch the Cowboys on TV and cook steaks. They put the steaks on foil and cooked them in the broiler in the house. Once the steaks were done, they loaded up their plates and headed to the TV. Shortly after they sat down, they heard a familiar noise from the kitchen. They got up and went into the kitchen, realizing they had left the foil-covered broiler pan out on top of the stove after removing their steaks.

When they returned to the noise they had heard, it was the roller pan that had been scraped and torn up, and the foil, which they had used to cover the pan before they cooked the steaks, had been ripped up. The tears in the foil were large, and the rat had clawed the foil all up. But he was nowhere in sight. The girls started looking for him, checking all the traps they had set, and there was no rat.

Mattie walked past the 3-foot-tall trash can in the kitchen and gave it a little kick. There was no cover on the trash can, and this rat flew out of nowhere in a flash. It scared both the girls, and they screamed, running out of the kitchen. He jumped from the trash can over the fridge, fell behind it, and was *gone.*

That night, the girls had some tequila shots with friends, and Mattie announced she was drunk and going to bed. She laid down and thought that *"rat better not come into my room."* Mattie's bed was against the bay window in that room, and all of a sudden, she heard his nails walking in that bay window. Click. Click. Click. Before she could think of anything else, she heard him jump down to the sheet on the bed. Dump. And it was a loud dump.

Without thinking, Mattie flew out of bed, grabbed her purse, and headed for the car. She never looked back that night. She got sober *fast.* Mattie never returned to the trailer. She had Renee bring her all her stuff, moving to a little apartment.

CHAPTER 8

THE COMPROMISED APARTMENT

Mattie started living in that little apartment and wasn't there very long, either. She moved in and was there for about three weeks when she had a customer who wanted some weed.

Mattie had gotten 25 lbs. of weed, and if she misted it with water, she could pull an extra 5 lbs. out of it. The guy delivered 25 lbs, and Mattie went and got a shower curtain liner and laid it open on the living room floor so she could sip through the weed and mist it as she went. This added water to the weed and weight, helping her to make more profit.

As soon as she got started there was a knock at the front door. She put the chain on and cracked the door open. It was her mother. She had just dropped by to visit. Mattie opened the door and invited her in. When Mattie's mom saw all that pile of weed, she gasped—looking at Mattie with her mouth open.

Mattie's mother had never seen so much weed before, so she started explaining how she had to work and apologizing to her mother for the surprise. She wasn't expecting her mother to stop by unexpectedly, and her mother looked worried. Mattie explained that it would only take 30 to 45 minutes and would all be cleaned up.

Mattie's mother had not really seen it before, only reaping the benefits of having a daughter who made money by selling the weed. Mattie had paid for her mother to go to Jamaica one year on her profits with a friend. And she once had her mother's home furnished with a ceiling fans for her birthday, which included 11 fans.

They were top-of-the-line fans, coming with lifetime warranties. She was also known to give her mom 1,000 dollars at a time when she needed it, and sometimes when she didn't need it. There was plenty of money to go around, Mattie thought, which was a way of life for Mattie. Her mom sat down, watching Mattie sift the marijuana, stirring it up as she misted it.

The women were just chatting when there was a knock at the door again. Mattie told her mom to shh! As she went to the door, her mom had just told Mattie that she needed to be careful with this shit and that it could get her into trouble someday. Both women jumped at the knock, and Mattie spoke through the door, asking who it was.

The voice on the other side said, *"Maintenance."* Mattie asked, what they were there for, and the maintenance guy said, *"he was there to spray for bugs"*. There was no way Mattie would open the door with all that weed covering the living room floor. She screamed back through the door that she had no bugs, and that it wasn't a good time for them to spray.

The maintenance guy said, *"Okay"*, and Mattie thanked him. When Mattie turned around, the weed and her mother were gone.

She started calling out to her mother, but she didn't answer, Mattie. As Mattie walked through the two-bedroom apartment, yelling and looking for her mother, she eventually reached the master bathroom. Mattie pulled the shower curtain open on the tub, and there stood her mother looking like Santa Claus. She had picked up the liner by all four corners and slung it over her shoulder. And there she stood in the tub with all that weed. Mattie started laughing.

She laughed so hard at the sight of her mother's face. There she stood with the shower curtain over her shoulder with this frightful look on her face, not knowing if it was her daughter or the police. She would go to prison for the rest of her life, she thought. Stepping over the tub, she headed for the door. She set the liner full of pot on the bed. She turned to Mattie and said, *"I've got to go. I can't take all this stress,"* and out the front door she went.

Mattie was in tears, now laughing, and called out to her mom, *"Love you!"* Mattie got rid of all the pot except for half a pound. And she had a customer stop by saying he knew someone who wanted about 100 lbs. They could make several hundred each if they could get this deal off the ground. Now, the normal procedure was to take a picture of the pot, and the other party took a picture of his money, and they exchange pictures.

Once the pictures were exchanged, the deal was to begin. Mattie's friend came knocking at the door unexpectedly. When she opened it, he had a friend with him, and Mattie invited them inside, wondering what was happening. This was not normal protocol here. There was no need for the customer to be at Mattie's home.

Mattie let the two men in, knowing the exchange would not happen there. The friend said he wanted to try it first, so Mattie went and got a small bag so he could roll a joint. But he was being suspicious as he wanted to see one of the pounds. And Mattie looked at him in surprise, saying, *"I don't have the weed here."*

You never want to transport that amount of weed from one location to another. One can meet on the road, but not in your home. The guy told her friend he wanted to speak to him outside. They stayed out there for several minutes, and Mattie got worried. So, she called the man with the weed, telling him what had happened and what had been said. The big boss told Mattie she was lucky, that she needed to get out of there *ASAP,* because the guy had come to rob her!

The deal would not happen for that guy. Once he found out there was no pot, that it was down the street, and he wanted to rob her, thinking she would be a pushover. But he now knew where she lived and that she had access to that kind of quantity. He would be back. And now her apartment was compromised. She was at risk. He could return any time. That thought made Mattie grab her pistol and start down the stairs to her car. She saw no one.

Once in the car, she fled to the first phone booth; cell phones were not out yet. She called her friend, the one who brought the guy over, and he said the guy had robbed him of his money when they went to the car and shoved him out while the car was moving. The friend now had some cuts and scrapes on him, but he had his life. He lost all the money he had to invest in the deal, but at least he was alive. Mattie never returned to the apartment. Instead, she sent a few acquaintances to pack her belongings and put them into storage. Oh, what an adventure this was. One she didn't want to ever have repeated.

CHAPTER 9

CONNECTION TO MUSICIAN'S

Mattie was a woman of adventure. She always seemed to get involved in situations involving criminals, though, and this time was no different. She had a birthday coming up, and a surprise party was being arranged—*all for her.* Her big guy had rented a club, and his whole team was invited.

Mattie came decked out wearing all her jewels. She looked great riding in the limousine. When she arrived, she saw other limos with her acquaintances also dressed to the hilt. The others were behind her as she entered the club. As the club was packed. People were everywhere, and the dance floor was crowded. Mattie was shocked. The dance floor had casually dressed people. Who were these people?

Shorts, flip-flops, and barely dressed women. They were everywhere.

Once inside, Mattie was escorted upstairs to a table that hung over the dance floor. It was all elegantly decorated. Her group filled the upstairs. *Who were all these people below?* It was an open bar. Every drink was paid for, and just on her behalf. She was so excited with a live band. The host made his way to her table. Gleaming with excitement, she thanked him, and he opened his arms, showing her all this was for her. Even the band was part of the show. And she had never seen these band guys before.

The band leader was a big burley guy, who had a smile from ear to ear. At break time, he came to Mattie's table, introduced himself, and a friendship started. Mattie went on to be friends with him for the next 20 years. Mattie showed up at every club he played in, supporting his music.

She eventually became friends with his wife, and they all partied together. Steve was on the payroll too. As soon as they got acquainted, Steve became her new customer. Steve was a cash customer. When most transactions involved large sums of money, fronting products was regular business. Cash customers were not, And that's why it was important to Mattie to be a cash customer. *Why spend your money when you could spend theirs?*

The price might be higher, but you just charged more. However, Steve was independent, and he paid in cash. Having $10,000 to pay was not common. That's how Mattie latched on. That available cash was the kicker. So, Mattie undercut whatever he was paying to win his business.

Steve played with six or seven members in his band. This would be a new door, and new clients would bring more people and more money. This friendship would last a *lifetime.*

Steve was a heavy weed smoker, and eventually, this would land him in jail. Eventually, he was released and started a new life. Mattie did not have contact with him for several years. And then one night, she entered a club to have a drink after work and see what band was playing, not whose, but what band was playing. It sounded like Steve, but this guy was *slim.*

Steve had lost over 200 lbs. and wore slacks. He looked totally different. He saw Mattie walk through the door first. This club was in a small town. A lake town, to be precise, and Mattie had moved there. *Who would have ever thought they would both be in this little town at the same time?* It had a population of 3,500 people. Steve was much heavier then, when they met in Dallas 20 years earlier, so Mattie was shocked. She was so happy to see him. It had been 5 years since she had seen him, and he looked great.

She was used to seeing him in overalls weighing about 375 pounds. Now, he weighed around 170. She said, *"What happened?"* He explained he was no longer in the pot business; *he had switched drugs.*

Now he was in the methamphetamine business, better known as crystal meth. Doing crystal meth, he had lost all his weight, but he looked good. And Mattie had never heard anything good about this drug. It was cheap, and it attracted cheap people. The people who used this drug created a whole new wave of the environment, a new wave of drug users.

People could spend less than $50 and be up for days. Staying awake two to three days at a time, sometimes longer, their minds were altered. They were out there, not getting sleep for days. They thought *differently.* They were paranoid, and would trade and sell their souls for more speed. After that night, Mattie didn't see Steve much except for in the clubs, running into each other several times a year. That was one drug Mattie didn't wanna have anything to do with.

Eventually, Steve returned to prison for crystal meth. And another five to eight years went by before their paths crossed again. This time Mattie was still in the pot business. She had a partner named *Neil,* and kept telling her about his uncle, who could be potentially new customer.

Eventually, Mattie agreed to her partner. And he went to talk to his uncle. Mattie waited in the car. Neil came out to the car and said his uncle would invest, and Mattie was glad she finally was gonna get to meet Neil's uncle. As she ventured out to get new customers. He told her his uncle didn't want to meet anyone new, and that was fine with her. Then he said something that Mattie was shocked by. He mentioned his uncle's name, and Mattie felt tickled inside. She couldn't believe it.

She knew that *name.*

She jumped out of the car and said, *"Take me up there. I know him."*

Neil said, *"No, you will ruin everything."*

She laughed, telling Neil his uncle could pay them a lot more than Neil had negotiated. Neil said he would be small potatoes but a cash customer, and he was wrong. This was a cash customer, all right.

Mattie insisted Neil take her to the uncle. And when she walked into the apartment, Steve whipped her up in his arms and spun her round and round. Neil was shocked. He wasn't sure what was happening. His uncle was very private not wanting anyone just to stop by, and no new faces ever. But Mattie was not a new face to him. It was Steve; *he was out and was a cash customer, always paying as he went.*

Steve told his new nephew to go into the living room and that he would talk to Mattie alone in the bedroom. Mattie stayed about two hours reminiscing with Steve, and a relationship was reborn. And he was a cash customer. Neil sat quietly in the other room until Mattie returned. She said, *"Let's go."* And so they went to the car. She opened her purse showing that she had been given $5000. Steve always dealt in cash.

This business deal lasted another five years, so Steve got into trouble again and went back to prison. This time, he was gone for five more years. The big boss, Mattie, had met Steve through. He also had gotten federal time and was in prison now for the next *17 years.* This made Mattie change her ways. She was lucky never to have gotten in trouble, but those 17 years scared her.

CHAPTER 10

SUMMER ROMANCE AND POLO DREAMS

Mattie was a worldly woman. She had girlfriends, but most of them didn't like each other. However, the men were attracted to Mattie, and she had many male friends. Mattie met a guy who was a polo player.

He was from *New Zealand.* Jacque was 6'5" with dark hair, dark eyes, and a beautiful smile. Jacques fell for her immediately, and Mattie had never gone out with a sportsman, especially with an accent like that. Mattie was intrigued by Jacque, and his smile made you melt. When he pulled her up close, she would come off her *tiptoes.* Mattie was only 5 foot tall.

She and Jacque were a hot item that summer. He played with Mattie for the whole summer. Then one day, he told her he just couldn't play anymore. He was at the polo club, and polo was why he was in the states. Many people were counting on him, and Mattie's lifestyle was on the wrong schedule for Jacque.

He looked pitiful, telling her he couldn't party with her anymore. She respected him for telling her that his broken English was so *cute.*

He said *one more night,* and she threw her arms around him. They went to dinner—a quiet place, then, a little slow music where they could just hold each other. Mattie's heart was beating fast. Jacque ordered tequila, and the shots began. Jacque carried Mattie to bed that night, and they had hot, wild sex *all night.*

Mattie woke to someone passing at the foot of the bed. *Who was that?* Then again, from the other direction. *What's going on?* Mattie thought. *Where is Jacque? What time is it?* And again, someone walked past her bed.

Mattie started looking around. There were no clothes. The blanket she was covered with was rough and small. *What is this?* she thought. Now, men were passing the foot of the bed in twos. Then it *dawned* on her. She was in the bunkhouse with a horse blanket, and these were ranch hands.

The bunkhouse was filled with about 15 men, and Jacques's bed was next to the kitchen. Which meant the bathroom was at the other end of the bunkhouse. As the men woke up that morning, they went to the kitchen and of course, they had to use the bathroom. Parading back and forth past the bed, she sat straight up. *Oh my God. She had to get out of there. Where was her car? She had no idea whether she drove or Jacque did?* She needed to *escape.*

She saw her clothes folded in a pile. She grabbed them and started trying to get dressed. She had on a flashy sequin top with blue jeans last night. It would not be appropriate for an early morning attire, but she had to move *fast.*

The sun was not up yet, and she could sneak away. She hurried. Once dressed, she peeked left, then right, and dashed to the door she saw that would led out of the bunkhouse.

Once outside, she gasped. *People*, lots of people, balloons and horses. *Where was the car? Whose house or property was she at?* She had to find the car. Thank God it was not too far from the bunkhouse. She ran to the car door, flung it open, got inside, and started the *Corvette up.*

As she backed out, she almost hit a man on horse. As she put the car in drive and started to step on it, it was Jacque. He had a polo stick in one hand but waved with the other, and Mattie threw him a flying kiss. He smiled so widely, and she *floored* it.

Mattie never saw Jacques again. She thought of him from time to time over the years. But one thing was sure: *he would never forget the wild time he spent with her*. He would never forget that woman from Texas and his summer at the bunkhouse. Mattie laughed out loud and never looked back.

CHAPTER 11

LOVE ON THE ROAD

It was almost summer again when Mattie met her next encounter. He was new in town—a *Navy Seal.* Again, Mattie had never been with a military man. This one was a *real* man. At 6'6, with blue eyes and dark hair, his physique was *unbelievable.*

He was a confident man. He and Mattie made a great team. Together, they could sell ice to an *Eskimo.* This man was different than all the other men Mattie had known. He had never done drugs, he didn't smoke, and he really did not drink. He cursed only when he got aggravated. And he didn't care what Mattie did.

It *truly* did not bother him if she had a drink or one too many, either. Mattie changed while being with *Devin.* They worked from dawn to dusk, traveling from state to state, selling out of products daily.

Devin asked Mattie to get married. He would try to marry her in every state they entered, whisking her into roadside churches on a whim, not worrying about a license. Devin would make a game of it, carrying Mattie over his shoulder into pastors' offices and begging them to marry the two. Mattie was worried that one of these pastors would say yes one day, even without a license. But the game kept getting played.

Devin was a romantic. He was always petting Mattie, *something she did not like,* and complimenting her on everything. Devin was such a large man at 6'6", and Mattie was so petite it was entertaining to watch them flirt. Mattie was happy with Devin.

The sex was *hot.* Devin would run a bath for her and excite her while she bathed. Running his big hand down her body while running his other hand down his body. Mattie would *shiver* with excitement.

Sex has always been different. It would always start as something sweet. From pinning her against a wall or a soda machine and licking her from head to toe. He was a great kisser. He spoke *dirty* to her, making Mattie giggle.

He would take her several times a day. He could always get an erection. Mattie stayed wet for him. *He couldn't keep his big hands off her.* Everything was so *perfect.* Mattie had never been so happy, but she knew something would go wrong, and *it did.*

Devin had no I.D. And Mattie had no proof of his identity. It didn't seem to matter much, but Devin would come in contact with the law periodically. Traveling state to state, he would make an illegal turn or something that would cause them to be pulled over. But Devin would always make friends with the cop.

With his military involvement, she would hear him reminiscing about Iraq. The police would be impressed with his tale or experience from the war, and they would always just let him go—no ID, no tickets, and a verbal warning about the traffic violation. *That was it, every single time.* Devin never got a ticket and never showed them his ID. Mattie thought this was strange, but didn't think anything more until the *very* end.

Mattie and Devin sold steaks on the highway—cases of meat. They had a chest freezer in the back of the pickup with a generator to keep everything frozen. Devin would unload all the meat boxes into their motel room, emptying the freezer. He would carry the freezer into the room and plug it in. Many nights, they had sex on top of that freezer.

One day, it was Mattie's birthday, and she was homesick. She wanted to return to Texas to be with family and friends on her birthday. But Devin said *no*, they needed to finish working on the territory they were in before returning. He promised they would celebrate her birthday. Mattie was all about *birthdays*. Mattie dressed up, not knowing what Devin had planned. At about 8 pm, he said, *"Let's go,"* They went to the little club they had been to every night that week while in this area.

Mattie was disappointed not to know anyone in this town, but they walked in, and the whole club was decorated with birthday decorations. All the patriots started singing *Happy Birthday,* and poppers started popping. Then came the bartender from behind the bar, carrying a birthday cake—a large sheet cake with lit candles—straight to Mattie. So, she could blow out the candles and make her wish. She couldn't believe that everyone in the bar was participating, and it was all for her. Devin had planned it all. And the *party* began.

Upside-down margaritas at the bar. Shuffleboard and pool tables, even a mechanical bull. Mattie really tied one on that night. She had bought the whole bar a round of drinks twice or three times, making bets on pool games. Devin was playing, and even she rode on the bull. She couldn't stay on it long, but kept trying, laughing so hard that her stomach hurt.

Devin may have had two beers that night, but Mattie lost count of her intake. She couldn't even remember leaving that night, but she remembered having sex with Devin. She had sex in the car, sex on the freezer, and finally in the bed where she fell fast asleep.

The next day, she had quite a hangover. She had a birthday party in a huge room full of strangers. But you know, Mattie, there were never any strangers to her. She made sure they all had a blast. She remembered that part. After work that day, she fell asleep in the car.

They had sold all their meat cases and had to go to Tulsa to get more. She slept the whole way. Devin and Mattie sold steaks for about a year on the road until Mattie slipped on some steps and sprained her ankle. She was laid up for six weeks on crutches.

While she was on crutches, Devin went to replenish the meat supply by himself and drop off the money they owed for the last shipment, but he never returned. He had about $4500 in cash and a full freezer of meat worth about $5000, and he hit the road.

The truck was a company truck, and he just stole it. He was gone about three or four days before he called Mattie. She was *heartbroken*. It was her job alone to start with when she took Devin as a partner. And now she had to answer to her boss about the truck, the freezer, the generator, the boss's money, and a freezer full of inventory.

Mattie had called a psychic the second day he was gone and recorded what the psychic said. She told Mattie he would never return. He would call and say he would send for Mattie, but she would never hear from him again. He would say he went to Mexico, yet he had gone in the opposite direction.

And that's exactly what happened. He said he loved her and would call back and send for her. But Mattie never heard from Devin again. She imagined hearing about him on *Oprah's* show or *Jerry Springer*. Nine women would be on the stage, saying they were engaged to him once, and all knew him by a different name because no one had ever seen his ID. She felt *used*.

Mattie stayed depressed for about four to six months over Devin, thinking, *was he really a Navy Seal? How many women had he done this to? Was he ever in Desert Storm? He sure had a lot of stories, but were they his stories?* Mattie never finds out the truth, and she doesn't date anyone for a long time after that. It put a real damper on her attitude. She didn't want to work either. She just *moped* around. Maybe it would have been different if she had not sprained her ankle. But Devin had planned on leaving; *was from the start*. He just didn't know when.

CHAPTER 12

WILD NIGHTS AND UNEXPECTED REVELATIONS

Mattie and Devin made a lot of money selling steaks most days, but Mattie missed that income, so she had to find a way to earn it again legally. And she *did*. Mattie took a bartending job. She was the only employee at the bar, and Mattie was making $700 to $1000 a night. She went all in on that job.

Throwing events to bring in more and more customers. She had a night when she brought in an 8-foot-tall bear for the customers to pay to wrestle the bear. They would win $100 if they could beat that bear, and everyone *tried*. No one could beat that bear.

One night, this guy got the bear dancing to the music. Swaying left and right with the music, the bear and he swayed on the third or fourth time; *down he went,* and the customers roared. The guy had beat the bear. So, Mattie had to find another event to keep the customers spending their money, and she did.

This event Mattie pulled off was a stripper. She came all decked out with long brown hair. The men *loved* it. The dancer danced all over the club, shredding her clothes. She was sitting on laps, kissing the men, when all of a sudden, she took off her bra, and the falsies fell out.

The men's mouths dropped open. *She had no boobs.!* The dancer was a man—cross-dresser, to be exact. Mattie got a kick out of this night, and the men got mad, rushing the cross-dresser out the back door. Mattie thought they were going to kill the dancer. The men got all hooting and hollering for about an hour and a half, and they were excited. When the truth was finally revealed, they felt insulted. Mattie was laughing so hard that she pissed her pants that night. She never hired another *stripper*, though.

READERS NOTE

Mattie Malone has many more adventures I'd like to share with you. She also has a love life and two children. Mattie has no siblings but has five aunts and uncles and five stepdads. Mattie inherited her mother's home, then inherited her fourth husband's home.

This provided a home for Mattie that she paid cash for. Her need for money never stopped, and tens of thousands landed in her lap numerous times. Insurance claims, a wealthy stepdad, and a thing called reverse mortgage.

Gave Mattie close to $500,000 in the next five years. I hope you aren't tired of reading because we are just getting started.

Look forward to book two!

www.ingramcontent.com/pod-product-compliance
Lightning Source LLC
LaVergne TN
LVHW010944110826
845149LV00013B/2751

* 9 7 8 1 9 6 6 4 1 8 4 9 8 *